Dramascri

A Christmas Carol

CHARLES DICKENS

Nelson

Thomas Nelson & Sons Ltd
Delta Place
27 Bath Road
CHELTENHAM
GL53 7TH
United Kingdom

A Christmas Carol – the script
© Guy Williams 1973
The right of Guy Williams to be identified as author of this play has been asserted by
Curtis Brown Ltd in accordance with Copyright, Design and Patents Act 1988.

Introduction, activities and explanatory notes by Penny Chatwin
© Thomas Nelson 1998

Designed and produced by Bender Richardson White
Typesetting by Malcolm Smythe
Cover illustration by Dave Grimwood
Black and white illustrations by John James
Printed in Croatia by Zrinski

This edition published by Thomas Nelson & Sons Ltd 1998
ISBN 0 - 17 - 432547 - 9
9 8 7
08 07 06 05

CONTENTS

SERIES EDITOR'S INTRODUCTION

Dramascripts is an exciting series of plays especially chosen for students in the lower and middle years of secondary school. The titles range from the best in modern writing to adaptations of classic texts such as *Oliver Twist* and *Silas Marner*.

Dramascripts can be read or acted purely for the enjoyment and stimulation that they provide; however, each play in the series also offers all the support that pupils need in working with the text in the classroom:

- **Introduction** – this offers important background information.
- **Script** – this is clearly set out in ways that make the play easy to handle in the classroom.
- **Notes** explain references that pupils might not understand, and language points that are not obvious.
- **Activities** – at the end of scenes, acts or sections – give pupils the opportunity to explore the play more fully. Types of activity include: discussion, writing, hot-seating, improvisation, acting, freeze-framing, story-boarding and artwork.
- **Looking Back at the Play** – this section has further activities for more extended work on the play as a whole with emphasis on characters, plots, themes and language.

INTRODUCTION

A CHRISTMAS CAROL, the famous tale of the stingy old miser, Ebenezer Scrooge and the ghosts who visit him one cold Christmas Eve is among the best-loved stories ever written. It was a spectacular success, selling six thousand copies on its first day of publication in December, 1843 and inspiring an immediate pirated version. Queen Victoria loved it, Dostoevsky, the great Russian novelist, admired it and Dickens, himself, laughed and cried over it more than over any of his other books. Today thousands of children continue to enjoy the conversion of Scrooge played out in lively film and cartoon adaptations.

Just as he was to do in his other novels, Dickens managed to slip snippets of his own experience into this Christmas story. He wanted to delight readers with light-hearted descriptions of the dancing and party games he loved but also to remind them of the poverty and hardship that he had experienced as a boy. The Cratchits' terraced house in Camden Town is reminiscent of his own boyhood home and Tiny Tim is very like his own nephew, Henry Burnett, a gentle and thoughtful boy, crippled from birth.

The book is a celebration, not just of dancing and parties, but also of generosity and forgiveness. And it seemed to have real influence on the actions of readers. One American factory owner gave his workers an extra day's holiday as a result of reading the book.

Whenever Dickens gave one of his many public readings to raise money for charity, *A Christmas Carol* was his firm favourite. This short and enjoyable script version of the story creates the fun of performance that Dickens loved whilst retaining the story's central concern with the mean-minded sinner, Ebenezer Scrooge and his conversion to cheery old gentleman concerned for the welfare of his employees and generous to the nameless poor.

THE CHARACTERS

CHARLES DICKENS *an energetic and successful writer in his early thirties.*

EBENEZER SCROOGE *a miserly and heartless old business man who hates Christmas and lives alone.*

FRED *Scrooge's nephew, a happily married and cheerful young man.*

A YOUNG BOY *(Scrooge as a lonely schoolboy).*

A YOUNG APPRENTICE *(Scrooge as an apprentice).*

A YOUNG LOVER *(Scrooge as he approaches the prime of life).*

DICK WILKINS *another apprentice and Scrooge's friend.*

SCROOGE'S FIANCÉE *a young woman in mourning clothes.*

OLD FEZZIWIG *a kind and gentlemanly merchant who employed the teenage Scrooge as an apprentice.*

THE GHOST OF JACOB MARLEY *Scrooge's former business partner who has been dead for seven years.*

THE FIRST SPIRIT *the Ghost of Christmas Past.*

THE SECOND SPIRIT *the Ghost of Christmas Present.*

THE THIRD SPIRIT *the Ghost of Christmas Yet to Come.*

BOB CRATCHIT *Scrooge's underpaid clerk and father of six.*

MRS CRATCHIT *Bob's wife and mother of six.*

MARTHA CRATCHIT *Bob's eldest daughter, apprenticed to a milliner.*

BELINDA CRATCHIT *Bob's second daughter.*

PETER CRATCHIT *Bob's eldest son about to enter the world of work.*

TWO SMALLER CRATCHITS *a lively boy and girl.*

TINY TIM *Bob's crippled child.*

A PORTLY OLDER GENTLEMAN *collecting for charity.*

FIRST STOCKBROKER *a business acquaintance of Scrooge.*

A SECOND STOCKBROKER

A THIRD STOCKBROKER

OLD JOE *a shady back street trader.*

THE FIRST WOMAN *Scrooge's charwoman carrying a heavy bundle.*

THE SECOND WOMAN *Mrs Dilber, the laundress.*

A MAN IN FADED BLACK *the undertaker's assistant.*

THE BOY IN HIS SUNDAY BEST

A CHRISTMAS CAROL
SCENE 1
Scrooge's Counting House

(We see, first, MR CHARLES DICKENS, who is to tell us this, the most famous of all his stories. He is dressed in the kind of clothes a very successful writer might be expected to wear.)

CHARLES DICKENS   Marley was dead, to begin with. There is no doubt   1
whatever about that. The register of his burial was
signed by the clergyman, the clerk, the undertaker,
and the chief mourner. Scrooge signed it. And
Scrooge's name was good upon 'change for anything
he chose to put his hand to. Old Marley was as dead
as a door-nail.

(SCROOGE appears. Being an elderly miser, he seems much thinner and shabbier than MR DICKENS.)

SCROOGE   Marley dead? Of course Marley's dead. And I know it,   10
don't I? How can it be otherwise? Marley and I were
partners for I don't know how many years, weren't
we? I was his only executor, wasn't I. His only
administrator, his only assign, his only residuary
legatee, his only friend, and his only mourner? Of
course I know that Jacob Marley's dead . . .

(He looks round uneasily.)

. . . But I never have painted out Old Marley's name.

---

executor, administrator, assign and **residuary legatee** *These legal terms explain that Scrooge had complete control over the terms of his partner's will.*

There it stands now . . .

(He points.)   20

. . . Years afterwards, above the warehouse door.
Scrooge and Marley. That's what our firm was called:
'Scrooge and Marley'. Sometimes people, new to the
business, have called me 'Scrooge' and sometimes
they have called me 'Marley' . . .

(He chuckles grimly.)

. . . I've answered to both names, haven't I? It's all the
same to me.

MR DICKENS   Oh! But he's a tight-fisted hand at the grindstone, is
that Scrooge! A squeezing, wrenching, grasping,   30
scraping, clutching, covetous old sinner! Hard and
sharp as flint, from which no steel has ever struck out
generous fire; secret, and self-contained, and solitary
as an oyster. The cold within him freezes his old
features, nips his pointed nose, shrivels his cheeks,
stiffens his gait; makes his eyes red, his thin lips blue;
and speaks out shrewdly in his grating voice. A frosty
rime is on his head, and on his eye-brows, and his
wiry chin. He carried his own low temperature always
about with him; he ices his office in the dog-days and   40
doesn't thaw it one degree at Christmas.

SCROOGE   *(In great disgust.)* Christmas! Ptchah! Christmas! . . .

*This descriptive passage uses strings of adjectives (**squeezing, wrenching, grasping, scraping, clutching**), similes (**hard and sharp as flint**) and alliteration (**s**ecret and **s**elf-contained and **s**olitary) to give a vivid picture of Scrooge.*

a frosty rime *a white covering of the frozen dew which lies on fields in frosty weather.*

The Dog days *– the hottest days of summer when the Dog star rises and sets with the sun (July 3rd – August 11th).*

(There is a timid tap, and BOB CRATCHIT appears. He is carrying a shovel.)

. . . Yes, Cratchit? What do you want?

BOB CRATCHIT   If you please, Mr Scrooge, the fire's quite gone out in my room, and it's cold, bleak, biting weather.

SCROOGE   Are you after coal again, Cratchit? I let you have a shovelful yesterday, don't you remember? You and I will find it necessary to part if you continue in this extravagance.   50

BOB CRATCHIT   *(Submissively.)* Yes, Mr Scrooge.

SCROOGE   Warm your hands over your candle, Cratchit. And put your comforter on. Then you won't be a drain on the firm.

BOB CRATCHIT   Certainly, Mr Scrooge. Thank you, Mr Scrooge.

(As BOB CRATCHIT prepares to withdraw, he is joined on the threshold by Scrooge's nephew, FRED who has walked so rapidly through the fog and frost that he is all in a glow.)   60

FRED   *(Cheerfully.)* A Merry Christmas, Uncle! God save you!

SCROOGE   *(With great scorn in his voice.)* Bah! Humbug!

FRED   Christmas a humbug, Uncle? You don't mean that, I am sure!

SCROOGE   I do. Merry Christmas, indeed! What right have you to be merry? What reason have you to be merry? You're poor enough.

FRED   *(Gaily.)* Come then! What right have you to be dismal? What reason have you to be morose? You're rich enough.   70

SCROOGE   *(Having no better answer ready on the spur of the moment.)* Bah! Nonsense! Humbug!

FRED	Don't be cross, Uncle!
SCROOGE	What else can I be, when I live in such a world of fools as this? Merry Christmas! Out upon Merry Christmas! What's Christmas time to you but a time for paying bills without money? A time for finding yourself a year older, and not an hour richer? A time for balancing your books and having every item in 'em presented dead against you? If I could work my will, every idiot who goes about with 'Merry Christmas' on his lips should be boiled with his own pudding, and buried with a stake of holly through his heart. He should!
FRED	*(Pleading.)* Uncle!
SCROOGE	*(Sternly.)* Nephew! Keep Christmas in your own way, and let me keep it in mine.
FRED	Keep it? But you don't keep it.
SCROOGE	Let me leave it alone, then. Much good may it do you! Much good has it ever done you!
FRED	There are many things from which I might have derived good, by which I have not profited, I dare say, Christmas among the rest. But I am sure I have always thought of Christmas, when it has come round, as a good time; a kind, forgiving, charitable, pleasant time; the only time I know of, in the long calendar of the year, when men and women seem by one consent to open their shut-up hearts freely, and to think of people below them as if they really were fellow-passengers to the grave, and not another race of creatures bound on other journeys. And therefore,

80

90

100

every idiot who goes about with 'Merry Christmas' on his lips . . .
Scrooge's hatred of Christmas is vicious.

Uncle, though it has never put a scrap of gold or silver in my pocket, I believe that it *has* done me good, and *will* do me good; and so I say – God bless Christmas!

(Carried away by the warmth of FRED'S speech, BOB CRATCHIT involuntarily claps his hands. Then, seeing SCROOGE'S face, he tries to pretend he hasn't.)

SCROOGE *(To his clerk.)* Let me hear another sound from *you*, and you'll keep your Christmas by losing your   110
situation . . .

(He turns to his nephew.)

. . . And you're quite a powerful speaker, Sir. I wonder you don't go into Parliament.

FRED Don't be angry, Uncle! Dine with us tomorrow.

SCROOGE I'll see you in hell first.

FRED But why? Why?

SCROOGE Why did you get married?

FRED Because I fell in love.

SCROOGE *(Growling, as if the idea is ridiculous.)* Because you fell   120
in love! Bah! Good afternoon!

FRED Nay, Uncle, but you never came to see me before that happened. Why give it as a reason for not coming now?

SCROOGE Good afternoon!

FRED I want nothing from you. I ask nothing of you. Why cannot we be friends?

SCROOGE Good afternoon!

FRED I am sorry, with all my heart, to find you so resolute. We have never had a quarrel, to which I have been a   130

	party. But I have made a real effort to be friendly, because it is Christmas, and I'll keep my humour to the last. So, a Merry Christmas, Uncle!
SCROOGE	Good afternoon!
FRED	And a Happy New Year!
SCROOGE	Good afternoon!
FRED	*(To BOB CRATCHIT.)* And a Merry Christmas and a Happy New Year to you, Mr Cratchit!
BOB CRATCHIT	Thank you, Sir. And the compliments of the season to you, too. 140
	(BOB CRATCHIT turns to let FRED out.)
SCROOGE	*(Muttering to himself.)* And there's another fellow! My clerk, with fifteen shillings a week, and a wife and family, talking about a merry Christmas. I'll retire to Bedlam!
	(A PORTLY GENTLEMAN now enters the office, and stands with his hat off, bowing to SCROOGE.)
THE PORTLY GENTLEMAN	*(Referring to a list.)* Scrooge and Marley's, I believe? Have I the pleasure of addressing Mr Scrooge or Mr Marley? 150
SCROOGE	Mr Marley has been dead these seven years. He died seven years ago, this very night.
THE PORTLY GENTLEMAN	I have no doubt that his liberality is well represented by his surviving partner . . .

I'll keep my humour to the last *Fred is full of the most generous and forgiving good nature, the very opposite of his uncle.*

Bedlam: *The Bethlehem Royal Hospital, an infamous London madhouse where the rich used to pay an entry fee to laugh at patients for an afternoon's entertainment.*

Portly: *'overweight'*

(SCROOGE frowns, shakes his head, and refuses to examine the credentials that THE PORTLY GENTLEMAN offers him.)

. . . At this festive season of the year, Mr Scrooge, it is more than usually desirable that we should make some slight provision for the poor and destitute, who   160
suffer greatly at the present time. Many thousands are in want of common necessaries; hundreds of thousands are in want of common comforts, Sir.

SCROOGE   Are there no prisons?

THE PORTLY GENTLEMAN   *(Taken aback by SCROOGE'S surly tone.)* Plenty of prisons.

SCROOGE   And the union workhouses? Are they still in operation?

THE PORTLY GENTLEMAN   They are. I wish I could say they were not.

SCROOGE   The treadmill and the Poor Law are in full vigour,   170
then?

THE PORTLY GENTLEMAN   Both very busy, Sir.

SCROOGE   Oh! I was afraid, from what you said at first, that something had occurred to stop them in their useful course. I'm very glad to hear it.

THE PORTLY GENTLEMAN   Under the impression that they scarcely furnish Christian cheer of mind or body to the multitude, a

---

liberality: 'generosity'

common necessaries: 'basic things we all need'

the union workhouses and the Poor Law *After the Poor Law of 1834, poor people were treated as criminals and confined to prison-like buildings called workhouses.*

The treadmill *a punishment for prisoners who had to turn a wheel by a constant treading action.*

few of us are endeavouring to raise a fund to buy the poor some meat and drink and means of warmth. We choose this time, because it is a time, of all others, 180 when want is keenly felt, and abundance rejoices. What shall I put you down for?

SCROOGE Nothing!

THE PORTLY GENTLEMAN You wish to be anonymous?

SCROOGE I wish to be left alone. Since you ask me what I wish, Sir, that is my answer. I don't make merry myself at Christmas, and I can't afford to make idle people merry. I help to support the establishments I have mentioned – they cost enough; and those who are badly off must go there. 190

THE PORTLY GENTLEMAN Many can't go there; and many would rather die.

SCROOGE If they would rather die, they had better do it, and decrease the surplus population. Besides – excuse me – I don't know that.

THE PORTLY GENTLEMAN But you might know it.

SCROOGE It's not my business. It's enough for a man to understand his own business, and not to interfere with other people's. Mine occupies me constantly. Good afternoon, Sir! . . .

(Seeing clearly that it would be useless to pursue his point, 200 *THE PORTLY GENTLEMAN withdraws. SCROOGE is about to resume his labours with an improved opinion of himself when a hungry boy, outside, stoops down at the*

---

abundance rejoices *'the well-off are celebrating'*

decrease the surplus population *'cut down the number of unwanted people'*

regale him *'give him enjoyment'*

keyhole to regale him with a Christmas carol. At the first sound of

'God rest you merry, gentlemen!
May nothing you dismay' . . .

SCROOGE seizes a ruler with such energy of action that the singer flees in terror. Then, he turns to BOB CRATCHIT, who has reappeared.) 210

. . . You'll want all day off tomorrow, I suppose?

BOB CRATCHIT   If it's quite convenient, Sir.

SCROOGE   It's not convenient, and it's not fair. If I was to stop half a crown for it, you'd think yourself ill-used, I'll be bound? . . .

(BOB CRATCHIT smiles faintly.)

. . . And yet you don't think me ill-used when I pay a day's wages for no work.

BOB CRATCHIT   But, Sir! It's only once a year!

SCROOGE   A poor excuse for picking a man's pocket every 220
twenty-fifth of December! But I suppose you must have the whole day. Be here all the earlier next morning.

BOB CRATCHIT   *(Joyfully.)* Oh, I will, Sir! I promise I will! Thank you, Sir! Thank you, Sir! I'll be off now, Sir, if you don't mind? . . . It's a long cold way to run, to Camden Town, with all this snow on the ground!

CHARLES DICKENS   And the clerk runs home to Camden Town as fast as he can pelt while Scrooge, growling fearfully, closes the office for Christmas. 230

WRITING: In pairs make a list of everything you discover about Scrooge from the opening scene. Share your findings with the class and begin a spider diagram on the character of Scrooge which you can add to as you read other scenes.

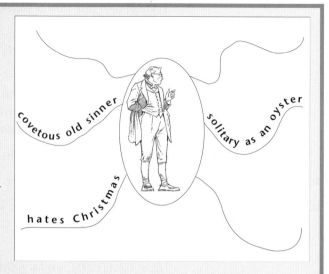

INTERVIEWING: In pairs read through the sections of script which involve Bob Cratchit and Scrooge. Plan and practise an interview in which one of you is a modern union official questioning Bob about his working conditions and his relationship with his employer.

WRITING: Write a short report of the interview for union records.

ROLE PLAY: In groups of four practise and perform a short television presentation on the subject of *Attitudes to Christmas*. One of you should take the part of television presenter and will need to introduce the programme, the theme and the guests. The others will take on the roles of Scrooge, Fred and Bob Cratchit.

You will need to read the text carefully in order to be sure of your character's attitude to Christmas. Be prepared to perform your presentation to the whole class, speaking directly to the camera with minimum use of notes.

EXPLORING LANGUAGE: This play adaptation of *A Christmas Carol* is shorter than the original but almost all the language comes directly from the novel. Re-read the speech on page 2 (beginning *Oh! But . . .*). In a pair list as many of the descriptive phrases as you can under the following headings:

	Appeal to sense of sight	Appeal to sense of touch
E.g.	A frosty rime	Hard and sharp as flint

SCENE 2
In Scrooge's Bare and Gloomy Chambers

CHARLES DICKENS	*(Continuing the story . . .)* It is later on Christmas Eve. 1 Fog and frost enshroud the old and dreary building in which Scrooge lives alone . . .
	(The sounds of distant Christmas music and ten or eleven muffled chimes can suggest the hour as SCROOGE enters.)
	. . . Before Scrooge shuts his heavy door, he walks through his rooms to see that all is right . . .
	(SCROOGE'S actions suit CHARLES DICKENS' words.)
	. . . Nobody under the table; nobody under the sofa; nobody under the bed; nobody in the closet; nobody 10 in his dressing-gown, which is hanging up in a suspicious attitude against the wall . . . Quite satisfied, he closes his door and locks himself in – double-locks himself in, which is not his custom . . . Thus secured against surprise, he takes off his cravat, puts on his dressing-gown and slippers and his nightcap, and sits down before the dying fire to take his watery porridge. Suddenly he starts up, as if he sees Old Marley's head in one of the wall tiles.
SCROOGE	Humbug! 'Tis humbug! . . . 20
	(Worried, he walks once or twice round the room. Then, he sits down again. As he throws his head back, a disused

cravat *a scarf worn around the neck, usually by men*
Humbug *Scrooge's favourite and scornful exclamation, meaning Nonsense!*

bell in the room starts to swing. It swings so softly at first that it scarcely makes a sound: but soon it rings out loudly and so does every bell in the house. When the bell stops ringing suddenly, SCROOGE hears a clanking noise, as if some person is dragging a heavy chain. The person seems to be coming upstairs from the cellars. Then he – or she – with the chains, comes straight towards the door of the room in which SCROOGE is sitting.) 30

. . . It's humbug still! I won't believe it! . . .

(SCROOGE'S colour changes, though, when the GHOST OF JACOB MARLEY comes into the room. The GHOST has a long chain clasped about his middle. It is made of cash-boxes, keys, padlocks, ledgers, deeds, and heavy purses wrought in steel.)

. . . How now! . . .

(SCROOGE'S voice is as bitter and cold as it ever was.)

. . . What do you want with me?

MARLEY'S GHOST	Much! 40
SCROOGE	Who are you?
MARLEY'S GHOST	Ask me who I *was*.
SCROOGE	Who *were* you then? You're particular, for a shade.
MARLEY'S GHOST	In life I was your partner, Jacob Marley.
SCROOGE	*(To himself.)* I have but to swallow this, and for the rest of my days I'll be persecuted by a legion of goblins, all of my own creation . . .

long chain *Marley's ghost is fettered by a chain of his own making. When alive, he spent all his time collecting and locking away money. Now in death he is weighed down by the symbols of his greed.*

ledgers *books in which accounts are kept*

shade *'a member of the spirit world'*

(He shouts loudly.)

. . . Humbug. I tell you . . . Humbug!

(The GHOST raises a frightful cry and shakes its chain   50
with such a dismal and appalling noise that SCROOGE
has to hold on tight to his chair to save himself from
falling away in a faint. When the phantom takes off a
bandage from round its head, SCROOGE falls upon his
knees and clasps his hands before his face.)

. . . Mercy! Dreadful apparition, why do you trouble
me?

MARLEY'S GHOST   Man of the worldly mind! Do you believe in me or
not?

SCROOGE   I do! I must! But why do spirits walk the earth, and   60
why do they come to me?

MARLEY'S GHOST   It is required of every man that the spirit within him
shall walk abroad among his fellow men, and travel
far and wide; and if that spirit goes not forth in life, it
is condemned to do so after death. It is doomed to
wander through the world – oh, woe is me! – and
witness what it cannot share, but might have shared
on earth, and turned to happiness!

(Again, the GHOST raises a cry, and shakes its chain, and
wrings its shadowy hands.)   70

SCROOGE   *(Trembling.)* You are fettered. Tell me why!

MARLEY'S GHOST   I wear the chain I forged in life. I made it link by link,
and yard by yard; I girded it on of my own free will,
and of my own free will I wore it. Is its pattern
strange to *you?* . . .

(SCROOGE trembles more and more.)

. . . Or would you know the weight and length of the
strong coil you bear yourself? It was full as heavy and

| | long as this, seven Christmas Eves ago. You have laboured on it, since. It is a ponderous chain! | 80 |

SCROOGE

(Imploringly.) Jacob! Old Jacob Marley, tell me more. Speak comfort to me, Jacob!

MARLEY'S GHOST

I have none to give. It comes from other regions, Ebenezer Scrooge, and is conveyed by other ministers, to other kinds of men. Nor can I tell you what I would. A very little more is all that is permitted to me. I cannot rest, I cannot stay, I cannot linger anywhere. My spirit never walked beyond our counting-house – mark me! – In life my spirit never roved beyond the narrow limits of our money-changing hole; and weary journeys lie before me! 90

SCROOGE

You must have been very slow about it, Jacob.

MARLEY'S GHOST

Slow?

SCROOGE

(Musing.) Seven years dead! And travelling all the time?

MARLEY'S GHOST

The whole time! No rest, no peace . . . Just incessant torture of remorse.

SCROOGE

You travel fast?

MARLEY'S GHOST

On the wings of the wind.

SCROOGE

You must have got over a great quantity of ground in seven years. 100

(On hearing this, MARLEY'S GHOST sets up another cry, and clanks its chain hideously in the dead silence of the night.)

---

ponderous *heavy and unwieldy*

incessant torture of remorse *Marley's language suggests that he is subject to the everlasting suffering and sorrow associated with Hell.*

MARLEY'S GHOST	Oh! Captive, bound and double-ironed! Not to know that any Christian spirit may find its mortal life too short for its vast means of usefulness! Not to know that no space of regret can make amends for one life's opportunities misused! Yet such was I! Oh, such was I!
SCROOGE	*(Faltering.)* But you were always a good man of business, Jacob.
MARLEY'S GHOST	*(Wringing its hands again.)* Business! Mankind was my business! Charity, mercy, forbearance and benevolence were, all, my business. That is why I am here tonight, to warn you that you have yet a chance and hope of escaping my fate. A chance and hope of my procuring, Ebenezer.
SCROOGE	You were always a good friend to me. Thank 'ee!
MARLEY'S GHOST	You will be haunted by my three spirits.
SCROOGE	*(In a faltering voice.)* Is that the chance and hope you mentioned, Jacob?
MARLEY'S GHOST	It is.
SCROOGE	I . . . I think I'd rather not.
MARLEY'S GHOST	Without their visits, you cannot hope to shun the path I tread. Expect the first, when the bell tolls one . . .
SCROOGE	Can't I take 'em all at once, and have it over, Jacob?
MARLEY'S GHOST	*(Ignoring this suggestion.)* Expect the second, on the next night at the same hour; the third upon the next

110

120

Charity, mercy, forbearance and benevolence *This list of abstract nouns of Latin origin covers the Christian virtues of love, pity, patience and kindness. Marley regrets that he didn't pay more attention to these when he was alive.*

of my procuring *that I have brought about.*

night when the last stroke of twelve has ceased to   130
vibrate. Look to see me no more; and look that, for
your own sake, you remember what has passed
between us!

When it has spoken these words, MARLEY'S GHOST
fades silently away. SCROOGE, desperate in his curiosity,
examines the door through which MARLEY'S GHOST
appears to have passed.)

SCROOGE   Double-locked, still . . . Just as I locked it, with these
two hands of mine . . . And the bolts are undisturbed!

CHARLES DICKENS   Scrooge tries to say 'Humbug!' but he   140
stops at the first syllable. Being, from
the emotions he has undergone,
or the fatigues of the day, or his
glimpse of the invisible world, or
the lateness of the hour,
much in need of repose, he
lies down, without
undressing, and falls asleep
upon the instant.

(Again, SCROOGE times his actions   150
to suit CHARLES DICKENS' words.)

WRITING: The ghostly atmosphere of this scene is created at least
partly through the sound effects. Read
carefully through the stage
directions for the scene. They are
written in *italics*.

Write a schedule of sound effects for the stage
manager and sound technician. For example:

> Sound Effects
> ────
> Sounds of distant Christmas
> music and 10 or 11 muffled
> chimes- As SCROOGE entens.

PERFORMING: Working in a group of three
or four make a radio recording of this scene. Two members of the group should
practise and perfect the reading while the remaining one or two carry out the role
of sound technician(s).

SCENE 3
The Ghost of Christmas Past

(SCROOGE wakes, as the chimes of a neighbouring church strike the four quarters. Then, he listens for the hour. To his great astonishment, the heavy bell goes on regularly up to twelve. Then, it stops. Twelve! It was past two when he went to sleep. The clock is wrong. An icicle must have got into the works. Twelve!)

SCROOGE   Twelve! Why, it isn't possible! I have slept through a   1
whole day and far into another night . . .

(He remembers the GHOST OF JACOB MARLEY.)

. . . Was it . . . Was it a dream or was it not? . . .

(The clock strikes again. SCROOGE counts.)

. . . A quarter past . . .

(And again.)

. . . Half past! . . .

(And again.)

. . . A quarter to it! . . .   10

(And again.)

. . . The hour itself! And nothing else! . . .

(Starting up into a half-recumbent attitude, SCROOGE finds himself face to face with another unearthly visitor. This one wears a tunic of shining white, trimmed with

---

 a half-recumbent attitude *half way between lying and sitting*

---

summer flowers. In THE FIRST SPIRIT'S hand, there is a bunch of fresh green holly.)

. . . Are you the spirit, Sir, whose coming was foretold to me?

THE FIRST SPIRIT	*(In a soft and gentle voice, as if it is speaking from a great distance.)* I am! 20
SCROOGE	Who, and what, are you?
THE FIRST SPIRIT	I am the Ghost of Christmas Past.
SCROOGE	Long past?
THE FIRST SPIRIT	No. Your past.
SCROOGE	What . . . What business brings you here?
THE FIRST SPIRIT	Your welfare!
SCROOGE	I am much obl . . .
THE FIRST SPIRIT	*(Clasping him, with its strong hand, by the arm.)* Rise! Rise and walk with me! 30

(THE FIRST SPIRIT'S grasp, though gentle, is not to be resisted. Scrooge rises. Finding that the SPIRIT is trying to take him away, he clasps its robe, as if he is pleading with it.)

SCROOGE	I am a mortal, and liable to fall.
THE FIRST SPIRIT	Bear but a touch of my hand there . . .

(THE FIRST SPIRIT lays its hand upon SCROOGE'S heart.)

. . . And you shall he upheld in more than this! . . .

CHARLES DICKENS	The Spirit leads Scrooge from his present-day dwelling 40 to another place, that he has almost forgotten.

(THE FIRST SPIRIT moves a small desk to the centre of the stage or acting area.)

THE FIRST SPIRIT	*(Returning to SCROOGE.)* Do you know where we are?
SCROOGE	*(Clasping his hands together as he looks about him.)* Good heavens! I was bred in this place! I was a boy here! . . .
	(He sniffs.)
	. . . And there are a thousand familiar odours floating in the air.

50

THE FIRST SPIRIT	*(As if to itself.)* Each one connected with a thousand thoughts, and hopes, and joys, and cares long, long forgotten! . . .
	(The SPIRIT gazes at SCROOGE mildly.)
	. . . Your lip is trembling. And what is that upon your cheek?
SCROOGE	*(Muttering, with an unusual catching in his voice.)* 'Tis nothing . . . 'Tis just a pimple, I expect . . . Come, show me what you will.
THE FIRST SPIRIT	I am showing you the school you attended, when you were a boy . . .

60

	(SCROOGE'S cold eye becomes dull again.)
	. . . The school is not quite deserted. A solitary child, neglected by his friends, is left there still, although it is Christmas.
SCROOGE	I knew it! I knew you would show me that! . . .
	(And as THE YOUNG BOY appears, representing his former self, SCROOGE starts to sob. THE YOUNG BOY,

odours *'smells'*

his lip is trembling, unusual catching in his voice *and* **his cold eye becomes dull** *These are the first signs of any emotion other than fear and bitter anger in Scrooge.*

lonely but self-sufficient, settles down to read, as if near a   70
feeble fire.)

. . . That's my poor forgotten self, as I used to be! . . .
I know! . . . Yes, yes, I know! . . . One Christmas time,
when that solitary child was left here all alone, in this
melancholy room, with nothing but his books for
comfort, Ali Baba came to keep him company . . .
And Valentine, and his wild brother . . . And
Robinson Crusoe . . . And there's the parrot! . . .

(*SCROOGE points wildly, as if he can actually see
Crusoe's bird.*)

. . . Green body and yellow tail, with a thing like a   80
lettuce growing out of the top of his head . . . There
he is! . . . And there goes Man Friday, running for his
life to the little creek! Hollo! Hollo! . . .

(*THE YOUNG BOY disappears, unhappily. As he does so,
Scrooge starts crying again, in pity for his former self.*)

. . . Poor boy! Poor boy! I wish . . .

(*He puts his hand in his pocket, finds no handkerchief,
and tries to dry his eyes with his cuff.*)

. . . But it's too late now.

THE FIRST SPIRIT   What is the matter?   90

SCROOGE   Nothing . . . Nothing . . .

Ali Baba *a character from one of the most famous tales of the* Thousand
and One Arabian Nights.

Valentine, and his wild brother *a French legend. Orsin was carried off
by a bear when still a baby and became a wild man but was later reclaimed
by Valentine.*

Robinson Crusoe *This is a famous adventure story written in 1719 by
Daniel Defoe about a castaway who leads a solitary existence until he meets
Man Friday.*

(He remembers something, and the memory hurts.)

. . . There was a boy singing a Christmas Carol at my door last night. I should like to have given him something; that's all . . .

THE FIRST SPIRIT   *(Smiling thoughtfully, as it removes the desk.)* Now! Let us see another Christmas!

(An OLD GENTLEMAN appears. He is wearing a high powdered wig.)

SCROOGE   *(In great excitement.)* Why, it's Old Fezziwig! Bless his   100
heart, it's Fezziwig alive again! I was one of his apprentices!

OLD FEZZIWIG   *(Rubbing his hands, adjusting his capacious waistcoat, laughing and calling out jovially.)* Yo ho, there! Ebenezer! Dick!

(SCROOGE'S former self appears again. Now, he is wearing clothes that suggest that he has grown a little older, and he is accompanied by the SHADE OF DICK WILKINS, who was his fellow apprentice at OLD FEZZIWIG'S.)   110

SCROOGE   *(To THE FIRST SPIRIT.)* That's myself, again! . . . Only, I'm a lot older! And that's Dick Wilkins, to be sure! Bless me, yes. There he is. He was very attached to me, was Dick. Poor Dick! Dear, dear . . .

OLD FEZZIWIG   *(To HIS APPRENTICES.)* Yo ho, my boys! No more work tonight! It's Christmas Eve, Dick. It's Christmas Eve, Ebenezer. Let's have the shutters up before a man can say Jack Robinson! Let's have a dance!

---

capacious 'large and roomy'

jovially 'cheerfully'

Let's have the shutters up *Wooden shutters were placed at the windows when business closed at the end of the day.*

	(With the two APPENTICES cheering this suggestion heartily, OLD FEZZIWIG skips away with wonderful agility.)	120
SCROOGE	*(To the SPIRIT.)* And he gave us a dance, too! I remember that so clearly! There was a great piece of cold roast, and there was a great piece of cold boiled, and there were mince pies, and there was plenty of beer. It did not finish until after eleven o'clock at night! Oh, we blessed him!	
THE FIRST SPIRIT	*(Coldly.)* A small matter, to make so many silly folk so full of gratitude.	
SCROOGE	A small matter?	130
THE FIRST SPIRIT	Why! Is it not? He spent but a few pounds of your mortal money . . . For that, does he deserve so much praise?	
SCROOGE	*(Heated by THE FIRST SPIRIT'S remark.)* It isn't only that, Spirit. He had the power to render us happy or unhappy; to make our service light or burdensome, a pleasure or a toil. Say that his power lay in words and looks; in things so slight and insignificant that it was impossible to add and count 'em up . . . But . . . But . . .	140
	(SCROOGE nearly chokes with emotion.)	
	. . . The happiness he gave us was quite as great as if it had cost a fortune . . .	
	(SCROOGE feels THE FIRST SPIRIT'S glance, and stops speaking.)	

Before a man can say Jack Robinson *This expression is believed to refer to an excitable gentleman called Jack Robinson who made flying visits.*

He had the power to render us happy or unhappy *Scrooge recognises that Fezziwig had qualities that were more important than wealth.*

THE FIRST SPIRIT	What is the matter?
SCROOGE	Nothing particular.
THE FIRST SPIRIT	*(Insisting.)* Something, I think?
SCROOGE	No . . . No . . . I should like to be able to say a word or two to my clerk just now . . . That's all.

150

THE FIRST SPIRIT	My time grows short . . . Quick!
CHARLES DICKENS	Again Scrooge sees himself. . .

(ANOTHER YOUNG MAN appears, representing SCROOGE at a later stage of his development.)

. . . He is older, now . . . A man reaching the prime of life. The face of the Ebenezer who appears before him has not the harsh and rigid lines of the Scrooge-face of later years, but it has begun to wear the signs of care and avarice . . . There is an eager, greedy, restless motion in its eye which shows that a certain passion 160 has taken root. It shows, too, where the shadow of the growing tree will fall.

SCROOGE	That's . . . That's me again!
CHARLES DICKENS	The young man is not alone.

(A YOUNG GIRL appears. She is dressed in black and is, apparently, mourning someone she has loved sincerely, and has now lost.)

SCROOGE	And . . . And I know that girl! . . . I know her! . . . We . . . We were engaged to be married, once upon a time.

170

SCROOGE'S FIANCÉE	*(To THE YOUNG MAN.)* It matters little . . . To you,

---

 avarice *'a greedy desire for money'*

---

	very little . . . Another idol has displaced me; and if it can cheer and comfort you in time to come, as I would have tried to do, I have no just cause to grieve.
THE YOUNG MAN	What idol has displaced you?
SCROOGE'S FIANCÉE	A golden one.
THE YOUNG MAN	This is the even-handed dealing of the world! There is nothing on which it is so hard as poverty; and there is nothing it professes to condemn with such severity as the pursuit of wealth!

180

SCROOGE'S FIANCÉE	You fear the world too much! I have seen your nobler aspirations fall off one by one, until the master-passion, gain, engrosses you . . . Have I not?
THE YOUNG MAN	What then? Even if I have grown so much wiser, what then? I am not changed towards you . . . Am I?
SCROOGE'S FIANCÉE	Our contract is an old one . . . It was made when we were both poor, and content to be so, until, in good season, we could improve our worldly fortune by our patient industry . . . You *are* changed . . . When it was made, you were another man.

190

THE YOUNG MAN	*(Impatiently.)* I was a boy . . .
SCROOGE'S FIANCÉE	Your own feeling tells you that you were not what you are . . . I am . . . Then, we were one in heart. Now, we are two . . . How often and how keenly I have thought of this, I will not say. It is enough that I *have* thought of it, and can release you.

Another idol *and* **golden** *This idol is clearly money which has begun to corrupt the nature of Scrooge.*

nobler aspirations *'finer hopes and ambitions'*

our patient industry *'all the hard work carried out together without complaint'*

THE YOUNG MAN	Have I ever sought release?
SCROOGE'S FIANCÉE	In words? No. Never.
THE YOUNG MAN	In what, then?
SCROOGE'S FIANCÉE	In a changed nature . . . In an altered spirit . . . In 200 another atmosphere of life . . . With another hope as its great end . . . In everything that made my love of any worth or value in your sight . . . If this had never been between us, tell me, would you seek me out and try to win me now? . . . Ah, no!
THE YOUNG MAN	You think not.
SCROOGE'S FIANCÉE	I would gladly think otherwise if I could, Heaven knows! . . . But if you were free today, tomorrow, yesterday, can even I believe that you would choose a dowerless girl? . . . If, for a moment, you were false 210 enough to your one guiding principle to do so, do I not know that your repentance and regret would surely follow? . . . I do . . . And I release you . . . With a full heart, for the love of him you once were . . .
	(THE YOUNG MAN tries to speak, but THE YOUNG WOMAN does not wish to hear him. She carries on.)
	. . . You may have pain in this . . . The memory of what is past half makes me hope you will . . . A very, very brief time, and you will dismiss the recollection of it gladly, as an unprofitable dream, from which, 220

---

a dowerless girl *'without title, rank or property.' The implication is that Scrooge would rather marry a rich widow.*

your one guiding principle *'the only belief that you live by.' She means his belief in the importance of money.*

repentance *'change of heart'*

dismiss the recollection *'force yourself to forget'*

fortunately, you awoke . . . May you be happy in the life you have chosen!

(THE YOUNG WOMAN leaves THE YOUNG MAN. THE YOUNG MAN goes vainly after her.)

SCROOGE   *(To THE FIRST SPIRIT.)* Spirit! Show me no more! Conduct me home! Why do you delight to torture me?

THE FIRST SPIRIT   One shadow more!

SCROOGE   No more! No more! I don't wish to see it! Show me no more! . . .   230

(Relentlessly, THE FIRST SPIRIT pinions SCROOGE'S arms and forces him to look into the furthest distance.)

. . . No! No! . . . I see that same young woman married happily to somebody else . . . I see her with more children around her than I can count . . . And, they are all so happy, together . . . They are having a Christmas party, and they are all laughing . . . This, I cannot bear! . . . Spirit! . . . Remove me from this place!

THE FIRST SPIRIT   I told you that I would show you the things that have   240 been . . . For what they are, do not blame me!

SCROOGE   Remove me! . . . I cannot bear it! . . .

(He turns on THE FIRST SPIRIT and wrestles with it.)

. . . Leave me! . . . Take me back! . . . Haunt me no longer!

(Somehow, SCROOGE manages to overcome THE FIRST SPIRIT completely, so that THE FIRST SPIRIT is forced to disappear. Then, exhausted by the struggle, SCROOGE sinks to the ground and falls into a heavy sleep.)

DISCUSSION: There is plenty of information about the character of Scrooge in this scene. You are told, for example, that he was a solitary child, neglected by his friends.

In a pair discuss and list everything you discover about Scrooge from this scene. Add new information to your spider diagram on the character of Scrooge.

WRITING: The Ghost of Christmas Past gives Scrooge glimpses of key moments in his past. Each moment has been important in shaping the character of the man.

In a pair plan and write an addition to this scene in which Scrooge is shown a different key moment from his past. Remember to include stage directions.

PERFORMING: Practise reading through your new scene and be prepared to present it to the rest of the class.

WRITING: Read through the exchange between the young woman and Scrooge in which she talks of their earlier relationship and the change in him.

Write a letter from the young woman to Scrooge in which she explains why she wishes to end their relationship and to release him from his promise to marry her. Use the formal and dignified tone of the young woman's speech in your letter.

SCENE 4
The Ghost of Christmas Present

(SCROOGE wakes, again as the chimes of the neighbouring church strike, first, the four quarters, and then the hour of one . . . When no Spirit appears he is taken with a violent fit of trembling . . . He gets up, softly . . . He starts to shuffle in his slippers towards the door . . . The moment his hand is on the lock, he hears a strange voice.)

THE SECOND SPIRIT	Scrooge! . . . *(SCROOGE nearly jumps out of his skin with surprise.)*	1

. . . Come to me, Scrooge! . . . Come to me, and know me better, man! . . .

(THE SECOND SPIRIT, clothed in a deep green robe, and wearing a wreath of holly on its head, materialises slowly. The SPIRIT'S eyes are clear and kind, but SCROOGE does not like to meet them.)

. . . I am the Ghost of Christmas Present! . . . Look upon me! . . .   10

(Reverently, SCROOGE looks at THE SECOND SPIRIT.)

. . . You have never seen the like of me before?

SCROOGE   Never! . . .

(THE SECOND SPIRIT beckons to SCROOGE.)

. . . Spirit! . . . Conduct me where you will! . . . I went forth last night under compulsion, and I learned a lesson which is working now . . . Tonight, if you have

under compulsion *'being forced to'*

	anything to teach me, let me profit by it!	
THE SECOND SPIRIT	*(In a commanding voice.)* Scrooge! Touch my robe! . . .	
	(SCROOGE does as he is told, and holds THE SECOND SPIRIT'S robe fast.)	20
CHARLES DICKENS	And the Ghost of Christmas Present takes Scrooge through the city streets and past the well-filled shops, until they reach Bob Cratchit's humble dwelling in Camden Town.	
	(MRS CRATCHIT appears and sets a small family dining table on the stage of acting area. She is dressed but poorly, in a twice-turned gown, but she has decorated it for the occasion with cheap ribbons, which make a goodly show.)	
THE SECOND SPIRIT	Let us stop here and bless Bob Cratchit's four-roomed home . . . It is a poor home, but a happy one . . . Bob has only fifteen shillings a week to keep a family on – thanks Scrooge, to you!	30
MRS CRATCHIT	*(Calling.)* Give me a hand with this cloth, Belinda!	
	(BELINDA, her second daughter, runs in to help. She, too, is wearing ribbons.)	
BELINDA	Right you are, ma!	
MRS CRATCHIT	And what's that Peter of ours up to?	
BELINDA	He's mashing the potatoes, Ma . . . Aren't you, Peter?	
	(BELINDA'S brother PETER appears, with a saucepan.)	40
PETER	Eh, Ma! . . . Can't I go out in the Park for a bit, before we has our dinner?	

---

let me profit by it *Scrooge is eager to learn and to change.*

Bob Cratchit's humble dwelling in Camden Town *This is a terraced house like the one in Bayham Street where Dickens lived as a young boy.*

MRS CRATCHIT	What d'you want to go out in the Park for, just before you has your Christmas dinner, for pity's sake?
BELINDA	He's got his Dad's shirt on, Ma . . . Didn't you notice? . . . Dad said Peter could wear it today as he wouldn't be needing it for the office . . . He wants to go out into the Park, with all the fashionable nobs, to show his self off!
TWO SMALLER CRATCHITS	(*Running in, in great excitement.*) Ma! Ma! We can smell our goose cooking, Ma! Ma! We can smell our goose cooking, Ma! . . .
MRS CRATCHIT	That wouldn't surprise me, either . . . It's got sage and onion stuffing in it.
THE SMALLER CRATCHITS	(*Together.*) Sage and onion stuffing! . . . Oh, yum!
MRS CRATCHIT	Whatever has got into your father, then? . . . And your brother, Tiny Tim! . . . And Martha warn't as late last Christmas Day, by half and hour.
MARTHA	(*Appearing.*) Here's Martha, Mother!
THE SMALLER CRATCHITS	Here's Martha, Mother! . . .
	(*They dance round their elder sister.*)
	. . . Hurrah! There's *such* a goose, Martha!
MRS CRATCHIT	(*Kissing her daughter a dozen times, and taking off her shawl and bonnet for her, in motherly fashion.*) Why, bless your heart alive, my dear, how late you are!
MARTHA	We'd a deal of work to finish up last night . . . And we had to clear away this morning, mother!
MRS CRATCHIT	Well! Never mind, so long as you are come! . . . Sit ye

50

60

nobs *slang for* members of the upper class

Martha is allowed one day's holiday only at Christmas; this was normal in 1843.

down before the fire, my dear, and have a warm, Lord
bless ye!   70

THE SMALLER CRATCHITS No! No! There's Father coming! Hide, Martha hide!

(*MARTHA hides herself, as in comes BOB CRATCHIT.
His threadbare clothes have been darned up and brushed,
to look seasonable, and he is carrying his little crippled
son, TINY TIM.*)

BOB CRATCHIT (*Looking round.*) Why, where's our Martha?

MRS CRATCHIT (*Teasing.*) Not coming.

BOB CRATCHIT (*His high spirits evaporating.*) Not coming? Our Martha,
not coming? Not coming home on Christmas Day?

MARTHA (*Not liking to see her father disappointed, even if it be*   80
only in joke.) Father! Dear Father! Here I am!

(*She runs into her father's arms while all the rest of the
family cheer loudly.*)

MRS CRATCHIT Just fancy you thinking our Martha wouldn't be
coming home, Father! As if any of us Cratchits would
stay away from home on Christmas Day!

BELINDA (*To THE SMALLER CRATCHITS.*) Take Tiny Tim out to
the wash-house, you two, so that he can hear the
pudding singing in the copper!

(*THE SMALLER CRATCHITS take their lame brother*   90
away.)

MRS CRATCHIT And how did little Tim behave, Bob?

BOB CRATCHIT As good as gold . . . And better. Somehow, he gets
thoughtful, sitting by himself so much, and he thinks

the pudding singing in the copper *The copper was a large basin in
which water could be heated by a fire below; the whistling sound is the
sound made by the boiling water in and around the linen-wrapped
Christmas pudding.*

the strangest things you ever heard. He told me, coming home, that he hoped the people saw him in the church, because he was a cripple, and it might be pleasant to them to remember, on Christmas Day, who made lame beggars walk and blind men see . . . I think . . . I think . . .   100

(His voice trembles.)

. . . I think he's growing strong and hearty . . . I hope he's getting strong and hearty . . .

MRS CRATCHIT   *(Hearing TINY TIM'S crutch.)* Hush, Father dear, here he comes!

(The young members of the CRATCHIT family return.)

CHARLES DICKENS   So, the Cratchit family's sparse Christmas feast is assembled. While Bob Cratchit pours out some hot mixture from a jug into two tumblers and a custard-cup without a handle, which are the only pieces of   110
glass the family possesses, while Peter mashes the potatoes with incredible vigour; while Belinda sweetens up the apple sauce; while Martha dusts the hot plates; and while the Smaller Cratchits set chairs for everybody, not forgetting themselves, Mrs Cratchit goes to fetch the goose. When she brings it in, there are wild cheers – not wholly deserved, for it is surely one of the very smallest geese that have ever appeared on any table.

MRS CRATCHIT   *(To THE SMALLER CRATCHITS.)* You had better cram   120
your spoons in your mouths, you two, lest you shriek for goose before your turn comes to be helped!

who made lame beggars walk and blind men see *Bob Cratchit refers to Jesus Christ who is reported in the Bible as healing a blind beggar and a paralysed man.*

32

BOB CRATCHIT	And what a goose it is! I don't believe there ever was such a goose cooked before!
MRS CRATCHIT	There'll be enough for all of us, as long as we put enough apple sauce and mashed potato on our plates.
BOB CRATCHIT	Now then! Are all the glasses filled? . . .
	(Murmurs of 'Yes!', 'Yes, Father!', Yes!'.)
	. . . Before your mother takes up the carving knife, as she does on this great and memorable occasion once every year, I want to give you a toast . . . **130**
	(There are murmurs of 'A toast!' 'Yes!' 'Stand up, everyone!' 'Give us the toast then, Father!' and everyone stands.)
	. . . I give you 'A Merry Christmas to us all, my dears. God bless us all!'
ALL THE OTHER CRATCHITS EXCEPT TINY TIM	A Merry Christmas to us all! God bless us all!
TINY TIM	*(The last of all.)* God bless us, every one!
	(As the other members of the family cheer TINY TIM'S own tiny toast, BOB CRATCHIT holds the child's withered little hand in his own, as if he dreads that TIM may soon be taken from him.) **140**
SCROOGE	*(To THE SECOND SPIRIT.)* Spirit! Tell me if Tiny Tim will live?
THE SECOND SPIRIT	I see a vacant seat in the poor chimney corner . . . I see a crutch without an owner, carefully preserved . . . If these shadows remain unaltered by the future,

 It is likely that Dickens's crippled nephew, a gentle, thoughtful boy, acted as model for Tiny Tim.

none other of my race will find him here. What then?
If he is likely to die, he had better do it, and decrease
the surplus population. 150

SCROOGE *(Nearly overcome with grief at hearing his own harsh words quoted by THE SECOND SPIRIT.)* No, kind spirit . . . No . . .

THE SECOND SPIRIT Will you decide what men may live, what men shall die? It may be, Scrooge, that you are less worthy, in the sight of heaven, and less fit to live than millions like this poor man's child.

(SCROOGE bends before THE SECOND SPIRIT'S rebuke, but he recovers speedily on hearing his own name.)

BOB CRATCHIT Mr Scrooge! . . . Raise your glasses, everybody! . . . I'll 160 give you Mr Scrooge, the founder of the feast!

MRS CRATCHIT *(Reddening.)* The founder of the feast, indeed! I wish I had that nasty mean old Scrooge with us here! I'd give him a piece of my mind to feast upon, I would, and I hope he'd have a good appetite for it!

BOB CRATCHIT *(Mildly.)* My dear! The children! . . . It's Christmas Day!

MRS CRATCHIT It should be Christmas Day, I am sure . . . On which one drinks the health of such a hateful, mean, hard, unfeeling man as Mr Scrooge . . . You know he is, 170 Robert! . . . Nobody knows it better than you do, poor fellow!

BOB CRATCHIT *(Even more mildly.)* My dear! . . . It's *Christmas Day*!

MRS CRATCHIT I'll drink his health for your sake, and because it's

---

If he is likely to die, he had better do it, and decrease the surplus population. *These cruel words are a taunting echo of Scrooge's own words in the first scene of the play.*

Christmas, but I'll not drink it for his sake, not never . . .

(She raises her cracked tumbler.)

. . . Long life to him! A Merry Christmas and a Happy New Year! *He'll* be very merry and very happy, I have no doubt!   180

(THE CRATCHIT CHILDREN drink the toast after her, from a sense of duty, but there is no heartiness in their proceeding.)

TINY TIM   *(As usual, last of all.)* To . . . Mr . . . Scrooge!

(THE CRIPPLED CHILD sounds as if he does not care twopence for MR SCROOGE. The mention of SCROOGE'S name has cast a dark shadow on the CRATCHITS' Christmas Party.)

BOB CRATCHIT   Well done, Tiny Tim! . . . And now, Mother, are we nearly ready to begin?   190

MRS CRATCHIT   I'm just wondering if the pudding will be done enough . . .

THE FIRST SMALLER CRATCHIT   Suppose it breaks, Ma, while you're turning it out!

THE SECOND SMALLER CRATCHIT   Supposing someone gets over the wall of the back yard, while we're all in here eating the goose, and steals it!

THE FIRST SMALLER CRATCHIT   Supposing someone has took it already!

(A kind of panic seizes THE CRATCHIT FAMILY at the thought of such a terrible possibility, and they all rush out to the wash-house.)   200

SCROOGE   *(To THE SECOND SPIRIT.)* Spirit . . . You have grown older, while we have been watching the Cratchits . . . Your hair is gray . . . Are spirits' lives so short?

THE SECOND SPIRIT	My life upon this globe is very brief . . . It ends tonight.
SCROOGE	Tonight?
THE SECOND SPIRIT	Tonight at midnight . . . Hark! . . . The time is drawing near!

(The chimes of a clock ring the three quarters past eleven.)

SCROOGE	Forgive me if I am not justified in what I ask, but I see **210** something strange, and not belonging to yourself, protruding from your skirts . . . Is it a foot or a claw?
THE SECOND SPIRIT	It might be a claw, for all the flesh there is upon it . . . Look here!

(From the folds of its robe, THE SECOND SPIRIT produces two children. They are wretched, ragged and miserable. They should be a boy and a girl, but they are scowling, and wolfish. SCROOGE has never seen any monsters half so horrible and dread.)

SCROOGE	*(Starting back, appalled.)* They're . . . They're . . . **220**

(He tries to say that they are fine children, but the words nearly choke him.)

. . . Spirit! . . . Are they yours?

THE SECOND SPIRIT	*(Looking down at them.)* The boy is Ignorance . . .

(He indicates the girl.)

This girl is Want . . .

(He looks up at SCROOGE.)

Beware them both, and all of their degree!

---

wolfish *The children,* Ignorance *and* Want, *represent the great mass of uneducated and very poor children neglected by the society of 1843.*

SCROOGE	Have they no refuge or resource?
THE SECOND SPIRIT	*(Turning on SCROOGE with his own words.)* 'Are there 230 no prisons? . . . Are there no workhouses?' *(The bell strikes twelve; THE SECOND SPIRIT vanishes . . . SCROOGE looks round for the ghost, but he fails to see it.)*
CHARLES DICKENS	As the last stoke of twelve ceases to vibrate, Scrooge remembers the prediction made by his partner, Jacob Marley . . . Lifting up his eyes, he sees another solemn phantom . . . It is the Third Spirit, draped and hooded entirely in black, that comes like a mist along the ground towards him.

---

all of their degree! *the great mass of other children like them*

Are there no workhouses? *Again the spirit echoes Scrooge's heartless words to the Portly Gentleman in the first scene.*

HOT SEATING: In groups of four discuss the different ideas that members of the Cratchit family hold about Scrooge. Then each person take on the role of Bob, Mrs Cratchit or any of the younger Cratchits. Take the hot seat for two or three minutes while others in your group question you about your opinion of Mr Scrooge.

IMPROVISATION: Working in the same group of four, improvise a scene in which Mrs Cratchit, Martha, Belinda and Peter are waiting for Bob to return from the Counting House of Scrooge. Without Bob's presence, they will be free to voice their feelings about Bob's low wages. They might also express their fears about Tiny Tim's health and their worries about money. Plan and practise the scene using appropriate accent and expression. Be prepared to perform to the class.

DISCUSSION: The Cratchits have little money and few luxuries, but their Christmas is a joyous one. In a pair list the features of the Cratchits' Christmas: the clothes, food, activities, toasts, etc. For each item on the list, find a feature of a modern Christmas which is very different. For example:

    small goose – massive turkey

WRITING: Using the information about income, accommodation and the special features of Christmas given in this scene, write a short entry for a school history book headed *Christmas for a clerk's family in the 1840s*.

SCENE 5
The Ghost of Christmas Yet to Come

(Shrouded in a garment which conceals its head, its face, its form, and leaves nothing of itself visible except one outstretched hand, THE THIRD SPIRIT silently approaches SCROOGE. When it is near, SCROOGE bends down on his knee, for the very air through which this spirit moves seems to scatter gloom and mystery.)

SCROOGE

(Filled with a solemn dread by its mysterious presence.) I am in the presence of the Ghost of Christmas Yet to Come? . . .

(THE THIRD SPIRIT does not answer, but points onward with its hand.)

. . . You are about to show me shadows of the things that have not happened, but will happen in the time before us? . . . Is that so, Spirit? . . .

(THE THIRD SPIRIT appears to incline its head. That is the only answer SCROOGE receives. But he senses, with a vague uncertain horror, that behind the dusky shroud there are ghostly eyes intently fixed on him.)

. . . Ghost of the future! . . . I fear you more than any spectre I have seen . . . But as I know your purpose is to do me good, and as I hope to live to be another man from what I was, I am prepared to bear you company, and I will do it with a thankful heart . . . Will you not speak to me? . . .

1

10

I am prepared to bear you company and I will do it with a thankful heart. *Scrooge seems even more determined to learn and to change.*

(THE THIRD SPIRIT gives SCROOGE no reply, but its hand points straight before them.)   20

. . . Lead on! . . . Lead on ! . . . The night is waning fast, and it is precious time to me, I know . . . Lead on, Spirit!

CHARLES DICKENS   The Ghost of Christmas Yet to Come takes Scrooge to the heart of the city . . . To the Exchange . . . To where the merchants hurry up and down, and chink the money in their pockets, and look at their watches, and play with their great gold seals, and converse in little groups.

(One of these little groups forms on the stage or acting   30
area. Seeing that THE SPIRIT'S hand is pointed to these
men, SCROOGE goes forward to listen to their talk.)

FIRST STOCKBROKER   No . . . I don't know much about it either way. I only know he's dead . . . Old Scratch has got his own at last.

SECOND STOCKBROKER   When did he die?

FIRST STOCKBROKER   Last night, I believe.

THIRD STOCKBROKER   *(Taking a vast quantity of snuff.)* Why, what was the matter with him? . . . I thought he'd never die.

FIRST STOCKBROKER   *(With a yawn.)* God knows.   40

SECOND STOCKBROKER   What has he done with his money?

FIRST STOCKBROKER   I haven't heard . . . Left it to his company, perhaps . . . He hasn't left it to *me* . . . That's all I know . . .

waning *'drawing to a close'*

Old Scratch *an unkind nicknamewhich makes fun of Scrooge.*

snuff *powdered tobacco which is inhaled through the nose*

(THE STOCKBROKER'S little joke is received with general laughter, so he continues.)

. . . It's likely to be a very cheap funeral, for upon my life I don't know of anybody to go to it. Suppose we make up a party and volunteer?

SECOND STOCKBROKER   I don't mind going if a lunch is provided . . . But I   **50**
must be fed, if I am to be one.

(More laughter.)

FIRST STOCKBROKER   Well, I never wear black gloves, and I never eat lunch, but I'll offer to go, if anybody else will. When I come to think of it, I'm not sure that I wasn't his most particular friend . . . At least we used to stop and speak whenever we met . . . Goodbye!

(The three BUSINESSMEN stroll away.)

SCROOGE   *(To THE THIRD SPIRIT.)* Someone has died, Spirit? . . . Who has died? . . . Who was the friendless person   **60**
they were speaking of? . . .

(THE THIRD SPIRIT does not explain. Instead it glides on, and SCROOGE follows.)

. . . Where are you taking me, Spirit? . . . I have never been in this part of the town before . . .

CHARLES DICKENS   The Ghost of Christmas Yet to Come takes Scrooge now to an obscure part of the town where he has never previously penetrated . . . The ways are foul and narrow . . . The shops and houses are wretched, the people half-naked, drunken, slipshod, ugly . . . The   **70**
whole quarter reeks with crime, with filth and misery

---

an obscure part of town *In this description, Dickens uses a series of adjectives to create an unattractive picture of poverty:*

slipshod *'careless and dirty in appearance'*

. . . The Ghost takes Scrooge into a low browed,
beetling shop, where iron, old rags, bottles, bones and
greasy offal are bought and sold . . . The Ghost shows
Scrooge the proprietor of this miserable shop.

*(OLD JOE, a wicked back street trader, appears and tries
to protect himself from the cold air outside his shop. As he
does so a WOMAN WITH A HEAVY BUNDLE slinks in.
She is followed by A SECOND WOMAN, who also carries
a heavy bundle. A MAN IN FADED BLACK follows the
two women. All three of OLD JOE'S visitors are surprised
to see the others.)*   80

THE FIRST WOMAN	Look here, Old Joe, here's a chance! If we haven't all three met here without meaning it!
OLD JOE	*(Removing his foul old pipe from his mouth.)* Which of you was here first, then? I deals, in the order they comes.
THE FIRST WOMAN	I, the charwoman, was first, Old Joe . . .

(She points to THE SECOND WOMAN.)

. . . The laundress, here, was second . . .   90

(She points to THE MAN IN FADED BLACK.)

. . . The undertaker's man was third.

OLD JOE   Stop till I shut the door of the shop, then . . .

(He makes to do this.)

. . . Ah! How it skreeks! There ain't such a rusty bit of

---

low browed, beetling *cramped and dark, such as beneath an overhanging part of the building*

offal *worthless pieces of raw meat*

skreek *This is a slang or dialect word meaning the grating squeal of rusty metal. (The sound of this word is like the sound it is describing.)*

metal in the place as its own hinges, I believe; and I'm sure there's no such old bones here, as mine . . . Ha, Ha! . . . We're all suitable to our calling! . . . We're well matched!

THE FIRST WOMAN	*(Throwing the bundle down on the floor and looking with a bold defiance at her rivals.)* What odds, then! What odds, Mrs Dilber? Every person has a right to take care of themselves, hasn't they? *He* always did!
THE SECOND WOMAN	That's true indeed! No man more so.
THE FIRST WOMAN	Why, then, don't stand staring as if you was afraid, woman . . . Who's the wiser? . . . We're not going to pick holes in each other's coats, I suppose?
SECOND WOMAN	No, indeed!
THE MAN IN FADED BLACK	We should hope not!
THE FIRST WOMAN	Very well, then! That's enough . . . Who's worse for the loss of a few things like these! . . . Not a dead man, I suppose.
SECOND WOMAN	*(Laughing.)* No, indeed.
THE FIRST WOMAN	If he wanted to keep 'em after he was dead, why wasn't the wicked old screw more natural in his lifetime? If he had been, he'd have had somebody to look after him when he was struck with death, instead of lying gasping out his last there, alone by himself.

Line numbers: 100, 110

We're all suitable to our calling! *'We're all well matched to the jobs we do.'*

What odds, then? *'What difference does it make?'*

screw *This is slang for* a stingy, miserly person.

natural *'kindly and normal'*

SECOND WOMAN	*(Nodding.)* It's the truest word that ever was spoke . . . 120 It's judgment on him
THE FIRST WOMAN	I wish it was a little heavier judgment! And it should have been, you may depend upon it, if I could have laid my hands on anything else . . .
	(She turns to the old dealer.)
	. . . Open that bundle, Old Joe, and let me know the value of it . . . Speak out plain . . . I'm not afraid to be the first, nor afraid for them to see it . . . We knew pretty well that we were all helping ourselves to the old miser's things, before we met here, I believe . . . 130 It's no sin . . . Open the bundle, Joe!
THE MAN IN FADED BLACK	No! . . . No! . . . Look at my things first, Joe . . . I've got 'em here ready . . .
	(He produces his share of the plunder. Each piece is examined separately, and carefully valued, by OLD JOE.)
	. . . I've got the miser's seal here. It's a fine one.
OLD JOE	*(Looking at the seal.)* Not up to much . . . Say, a penny or two.
THE MAN IN FADED BLACK	And here's the old miser's pencil case.
OLD JOE	*(Looking at the pencil case.)* Nobody wants second-hand pencil cases nowadays . . . You can't give them 140 away . . . Shall we say twopence, because we're old friends?
THE MAN IN FADED BLACK	And here's the old miser's sleeve buttons.

seal *a device for stamping a design on letters and other documents*

OLD JOE	*(Looking at the sleeve buttons.)* If they were gold, or even silver, they might be worth something . . . As it is . . .
	(He shrugs his shoulders expressively.)
	. . . Might as well chuck 'em on the fire!
	(In spite of this inglorious assessment, OLD JOE tucks SCROOGE'S sleeve buttons carefully into his own waistcoat pocket.) 15(
THE MAN IN FADED BLACK	Oh, dear! . . . Well, here's the brooch the old miser used to wear.
	(He hands Scrooge's brooch to OLD JOE.)
OLD JOE	*(Looking at the brooch.)* Paste and pinchbeck, as one might have expected . . . Give you threepence for it, for old time's sake, though Lord knows I'll be out of pocket . . . Let's see . . . That's a penny for the seal . . . Two pence for the pencil case . . . And three pence for the brooch . . . 16(
	(He pretends to add up these large sums.)
	. . . Five pence, in all . . . I'm robbing myself . . . I wouldn't give you as much as sixpence if I was to be boiled alive for not doing it . . . Now, who's next?
	(THE SECOND WOMAN produces her share of the plunder. Once again, each piece is examined separately, and valued, by OLD JOE.)
THE SECOND WOMAN	Here's the old miser's sheets.
	(She hands SCROOGE'S sheets to OLD JOE) 17(

---

 this inglorious assessment *the mean way he undervalues Scrooge's possessions*

Paste and pinchbeck *cheap and worthless*

OLD JOE	*(Looking at the sheets.)* Stained and rotting . . . No use, even as rags . . .
	(He tucks them away in a safe place.)
THE SECOND WOMAN	Here's the old miser's towels.
	(She hands SCROOGE'S towels to OLD JOE.)
OLD JOE	*(Looking at the towels.)* I wonder what he'd been using them for? . . . We'd better get rid of them, quickly.
	(He tucks them away in another safe place.)
THE SECOND WOMAN	Here's the woollen comforter the old miser was wearing when he . . . When he . . . 180
	(She makes, discreetly, some sign of benediction.)
	. . . When he passed away.
	(She hands SCROOGE'S woollen comforter to OLD JOE.)
OLD JOE	*(Looking at the woollen comforter, which has been worn for many years.)* Bury it in the garden, something might come up . . . Give you a penny for it, on the off-chance, any how . . .
SECOND WOMAN	*(Offering to OLD JOE a pair of SCROOGE'S boots almost as reverently as she would have tendered to him, if she had been lucky enough to find them in SCROOGE'S death* 190 *bed, a pair of original carvings by Michelangelo.)* Here's the very boots off his feet . . .
	(As OLD JOE turns the boots over and looks at their well-worn soles, she adds:)

She makes discreetly some sign of benediction *Looking around cautiously, she makes the sign of the cross.*

As reverently as she would have tendered to him . . . Michelangelo. *She hands the boots over as carefully and respectfully as if they had been priceless works of art.*

... They're leather.

OLD JOE

(*Sadly.*) They were leather, Mrs Dilber . . . What's left of 'em . . . They're not worth anything now, my dear . . . The hide has perished . . . But I tell you what . . . As we're old friends . . . I'll allow you FOURPENCE, on the slate, towards the next lot of goods you brings in . . . From the next decent deathbed of the next decent citizen you can get your 'ands on . . . Right? . . . Not an old miser's deathbed . . .

200

(*A little bewildered, THE SECOND WOMAN appears to agree.*)

. . . I always give too much to ladies . . . It's a weakness of mine . . .

(*THE SECOND WOMAN appears to be a little embarrassed, but pleased, at this suggestion.*)

210

. . . And that's the way I ruins myself . . . So, that's your account, then . . . Fourpence, towards the next . . . If you asked me for another penny, and made it an open question, I'd repent of being so liberal, and I'd knock off two whole shillings, at least.

THE FIRST WOMAN

And now undo *my* bundle, Old Joe.

(*OLD JOE goes down on his knees so that he can undo the bundle more easily. When he has unfastened the knots, he drags out a large heavy roll of some dark stuff.*)

OLD JOE

What do you call this, eh? . . . Bed-curtains?

220

THE FIRST WOMAN

(*Laughing and leaning forward.*) Ah! Bed-curtains! What else?

---

on the slate *This is credit to be spent in the shop rather than cash-in-hand.*

liberal *'generous'*

OLD JOE	You don't mean to say you took all 'is bed-curtains down, rings and all, while that old miser was still lying there? . . . Before he'd been put in his grave?
THE FIRST WOMAN	Yes, I do . . . Why not?
OLD JOE	*(Half admiring her cleverness.)* You were born to make your fortune, and you'll certainly do it.
THE FIRST WOMAN	I certainly shan't hold my hand back . . . Not if I can get anything in it by reaching it out . . . Not for the sake of such a man as he was, I promise you, Joe . . . 230
	(She points to the bundle.)
	. . . There's his blankets, in here.
OLD JOE	His blankets? . . . The miser's *blankets*?
THE FIRST WOMAN	Whose else's do you think? . . . He isn't likely to take cold without 'em now.
OLD JOE	*(Anxiously.)* I hope he didn't die of anything catching? Eh?
THE FIRST WOMAN	Don't you be afraid of that! . . . I ain't so fond of his company that I'd loiter about him for such things, if he did. 240
OLD JOE	*(Taking a garment from the bundle.)* What's this? . . .
	(He examines it.)
	. . . A shirt?
THE FIRST WOMAN	Ay! You may look through that shirt till your eyes ache; but you won't find a hole in it, nor a threadbare place. It's the best he had, and a fine one, too . . .

---

loiter *'stand around'* or *'take my time'*

	They'd have wasted it, if it hadn't been for me.
OLD JOE	What do you call wasting of it?
THE FIRST WOMAN	(*With a laugh.*) Putting it on him to be buried in, to be sure! . . . Somebody was fool enough to do it, but I took it off again . . . If sacking ain't good enough for such a purpose, it isn't good enough for anything . . . It's quite as becoming to the body . . . He couldn't look uglier than he did in that shirt . . . Now, let's have the money for what we've brought you . . .

(OLD JOE produces a flannel bag with money in it and starts reluctantly to count out a few coins.)

. . . Ha! Ha! . . . This is the end of it, you see! . . . He frightened everyone away from him when he was alive, to profit us when he was dead! Ha! Ha! Ha!

(With wild screams of laughter, OLD JOE and the ghouls with whom he is dealing disappear.)

| **SCROOGE** | (*Shuddering from head to foot.*) Spirit! . . . I see! . . . I see! . . . The case of this unhappy man might be my own! . . . My life tends that way, now . . . |

(But THE THIRD SPIRIT is not listening to SCROOGE . . . Its steady head is pointing to something ahead. SCROOGE looks to see what it is indicating. He shudders even more violently.)

. . . What are you showing me?. . . Don't take me any further! . . . No! . . . No! . . . I see a bed . . . A bare, uncurtained bed . . . On it, beneath a ragged sheet, there is something lying, dumb . . . I know what it is . . . No! . . . No! . . . Take me away! . . .

---

 ghoul *an Eastern demon that feeds on the souls of the dead*

CHARLES DICKENS	Scrooge puts his arm over his eyes, so that he shall not be able to see the plundered and bereft, unwatched, unwept, uncared for body that the Third Spirit is trying to show him.
SCROOGE	If that man could be raised up now, what would be his foremost thoughts? . . . Of making money? . . . Of clever dealing? . . . No, never! . . . They have brought him to a rich end, truly! . . . Lying there, in that dark empty house, with not a man, a woman, or a child to say 'he was kind to me in this or that, and for the memory of one kind word I will be kind to him' . . .

(He stops speaking for a moment, as he hears a terrible sound.)

. . . Hark! . . . There is a sound of gnawing rats beneath the hearth-stone . . . What they want in this room of death, and why they are so restless and disturbed, I do not dare to think . . . Spirit! . . . This is a dreadful place! . . . In leaving it, I shall not leave its lesson . . . Let us go! . . .

(Still THE THIRD SPIRIT points ahead, with an unmoving finger.)

. . . Spectre! . . . Something informs me that our parting moment is at hand . . . I know it, but I know not how . . . Tell me . . . What man was that, whom we saw there, lying dead? . . .

(THE THIRD SPIRIT does not answer, but it propels SCROOGE rapidly forward.)

. . . This courtyard . . . Where my place of business

bereft *'abandoned'*; **unwatched** *'with no-one to sit lovingly beside it'*. The description of the body on the bed shows how Dickens liked to use strings of adjectives: **plundered** and **bereft, unwatched, unwept, uncared for**.

is . . . My office . . . It is an office still, but it is no longer mine . . . The furniture is different . . . The figure in the chair . . . That is not me . . . And what is this? An iron gate? . . . A churchyard? . . . Here, then, the wretched man whose name I am to learn lies underneath the ground . . . It is a worthy place . . . Walled in by houses . . . Over-run by grass and weeds, the growth of vegetation's death, not life . . . Choked   310 up with too much burying . . . Fat with repleted appetite . . . A worthy place! . . .

CHARLES DICKENS   The Third Spirit appears to stand among some graves, pointing down to one. Scrooge, trembling, advances towards the spot.

SCROOGE   *(To THE THIRD SPIRIT.)* Before I draw near to that stone to which you point, answer me one question. Are these the shadows of the things that will be, or are they the shadows of the things that may be, only? . . .   320

CHARLES DICKENS   Still, the Third Spirit points downward.

SCROOGE   *(To THE THIRD SPIRIT, again.)* Men's courses will foreshadow certain ends, to which, if persevered in, they must lead . . . But if the courses are departed from, the ends will change . . . Say it is thus with what you show me! . . .

CHARLES DICKENS   The Third Spirit is immovable as ever. Scrooge follows the direction in which its finger is pointing and reads upon the stone of the neglected grave his own name.

SCROOGE   *Ebenezer Scrooge!* . . . Am I that man who lay upon the   330 bed? . . .

Fat with repleted appetite *'full to bursting from overeating'*

Men's courses will foreshadow . . . *What happens to people after death depends on their actions in life. Scrooge believes that if people change for the better, what happens to them after death will also change.*

(THE THIRD SPIRIT'S finger points from the grave to SCROOGE, and back again.)

. . . No spirit! . . . On, no, no! . . .

(THE THIRD SPIRIT'S finger points immovably to the ground.)

. . . Spirit! . . .

(SCROOGE clutches tightly THE THIRD SPIRIT'S robe.)

340

. . . Spirit, hear me! . . . I am not the man I was . . . I will not be the man I must have been but for what has happened . . . Why show me this, if I am past all hope?

350

(For the first time THE THIRD SPIRIT'S hand appears to shake.)

. . . Good Spirit! . . .

(SCROOGE falls on the ground before THE THIRD SPIRIT.)

. . . Your nature intercedes for me and pities me. Assure me that I yet may change these shadows you have shown me, by an altered life! . . .

 Your nature intercedes for me and pities me. *Your kind heart is sorry for me and asks God to forgive me.*

(THE THIRD SPIRIT'S hand trembles visibly.)   36

. . . I will honour Christmas in my heart, and try to keep it all the year. I will live in the past, the present, and the future. The spirits of all three shall strive within me . . . I will not shut out the lessons that they teach . . . Oh, tell me I may sponge away the writing on this stone!

CHARLES DICKENS   In his agony, Scrooge catches the Third Spirit's hand. The Spirit, stronger than he is, pushes him away. Scrooge then holds up his hands in a last prayer to have his fate reversed. He prays so successfully that   37 the Spirit shrinks, collapses, and vanishes utterly away . . .

(THE THIRD SPIRIT is made to disappear.)

. . . Scrooge, exhausted, sinks once more to the floor.

IMPROVISATION: Old Joe, the back street trader, is a shady dealer. He talks down the value of the goods the other characters bring him and offers them very little money. In a pair improvise an argument between a more determined customer and Old Joe. The customer is desperate for money and certain of the value of the item he or she brings. Joe is reluctant to give anything like a fair price.

WRITING: In this nightmarish scene, Scrooge is forced to face his own death. In our society when an important person dies there is an announcement in the media and an obituary in a broadsheet newspaper. In a pair prepare and deliver a short item for radio or television news concerning the death of the wealthy but miserly businessman, Ebenezer Scrooge. Use the details given in this scene and add details of your own.

WRITING: Look back at the detail you have collected on Scrooge in the form of lists and the spider diagram. Write a short obituary for a broadsheet newspaper. Jacob Marley's might look like this. ➔

MONDAY, 27 DECEMBER 1886

O B I T U A R Y

JACOB MARLEY, who has died aged 70, was for many years a partner in the London Finance firm of Scrooge and Marley. He was born on 5th September 1816 and spent his years in the partnership's Counting House in Clerkenwell, London EC.

EXPLORING LANGUAGE: When Dickens describes the obscure part of town (p40), he uses the verb reeks, the abstract nouns crime and filth and a string of adjectives to stress the dirty and unpleasant nature of the place. List the adjectives that Dickens uses. For example: *foul, narrow* . . .

DISCUSSION: Old Joe and the two women use slang terms (*screw*) and non standard grammar (*ain't*) suggesting a lower social status. In a group of three re-read and discuss the language used by the Portly Gentleman in scene 1, the Cratchit family in scene 4 and the low-life characters in this scene. List all the examples of non standard English you can find.

WRITING: In the same small group write a short conversation between the Portly Gentleman, Old Joe and a member of the Cratchit family, using the right sort of language for each character.

SCENE 6
The End of It

CHARLES DICKENS (*Setting a tall upright post by the prostrate SCROOGE.*) Now, we shall see our hero wake from his long, long dream.

SCROOGE (*Rubbing his eyes as if he has been asleep for a hundred years, and focussing his gaze, with some difficulty, on the post that CHARLES DICKENS has just set up.*) A bedpost! . . . I thought I was with a Spirit, and it turns out . . . to be . . . Would you believe it? . . . A bedpost! . . . My own bedpost! . . . The bed is my own! . . . The room is my own! . . . Best and happiest of all, the time before me is my own, to make amends in! . . .

(*SCROOGE makes some wild movements with his arms, as if he is scrambling urgently out of bed.*)

. . . I will live in the past, the present, and the future! . . . The spirits of all three shall strive within me . . . Oh, Jacob Marley! . . . Heaven, and the Christmas time be praised for this! . . . I say it on my knees, old Jacob! . . . On my knees! . . .

(*SCROOGE is so flustered by his good intentions that his broken voice will scarcely answer to his call.*)

. . . My bed-curtains are here . . . I am here . . . The shadows of the things that would have been may be

  make amends *'put things right'*

dispelled . . . They will be! . . . I know they will! . . .

(SCROOGE, laughing and crying in the same breath, finds and tries to put on his most extravagant clothes.)

. . . I don't know what to do! . . . I am as light as a feather! . . . I am as happy as an angel!. . . I am as merry as a schoolboy! . . . I am as giddy as a drunken man! . . . A Merry Christmas to everybody! . . . A Happy New Year to all the world . . . Hallo, there! . . .   30
Hallo! . . .

(SCROOGE is now frisking round the rooms in which he lives.)

. . . There's the door by which the Ghost of Jacob Marley entered! . . . There's the corner where I first saw the Ghost of Christmas Present! . . . It's all right! . . . It's all true! . . . It all happened! . . . Ha! . . . Ha! . . . Ha! . . . I'm home again! . . .

(For a man who has been out of practice for so many years, SCROOGE laughs splendidly.)   40

. . . I don't know what day of the month it is . . . I don't know how long I have been among the spirits . . . I don't know anything! . . . Never mind! . . . I don't care! . . . Hallo, there! . . .

(SCROOGE is checked, temporarily, in his joyful outpourings by the sound of church bells ringing out the lustiest peals he has ever heard. He appears to run to a window, to open it, and to put out his head.)

. . . No fog? . . . No mist? . . . Clear, golden sunlight! . . . Heavenly sky! . . . Sweet fresh air! . . .   50

I am as light as a feather! *Dickens uses a string of similes to suggest Scrooge's new and joyous mood:* **as happy as an angel!, as merry as a schoolboy!, as giddy as a drunken man!**

Merry bells! . . . Oh, glorious! . . .

(He calls to THE BOY IN HIS SUNDAY BEST, who is loitering near.)

. . . Hi! . . . What's today?

THE BOY IN HIS SUNDAY BEST	Eh?
SCROOGE	What's today, my fine fellow?
THE BOY IN HIS SUNDAY BEST	Today? . . . Why, it's CHRISTMAS DAY!

SCROOGE
(Almost to himself.) It's Christmas Day! . . . Then I haven't missed it! . . . The Spirits have done it all in one night . . . They can do anything they like . . . Of course they can . . . Of course they can . . .

(He shouts again to THE BOY IN HIS SUNDAY BEST.)

. . . Hallo, my fine fellow!

THE BOY IN HIS SUNDAY BEST	Hallo!
SCROOGE	Do you know the poulterer's in the next street but one, at the corner?
THE BOY IN HIS SUNDAY BEST	I should jolly well hope so!

SCROOGE
An intelligent boy! . . . A remarkable boy! . . . Do you know whether they've sold the prize turkey that was hanging up there? . . . Not the *little* prize turkey . . . The big one?

THE BOY IN HIS SUNDAY BEST	What, the one as big as me?
SCROOGE	What a delightful boy! . . . It's a pleasure to talk to him! . . . Yes, my grand lad!

THE BOY IN HIS SUNDAY BEST	It's hanging there now!
SCROOGE	Is it? . . . Go and buy it!
THE BOY IN HIS SUNDAY BEST	You're joking . . . YOU'RE JO. . .KING!
SCROOGE	No! . . . No! . . . I am in earnest! . . . Go and buy it, and bring it here, so that I can tell 'em where to take it . . . Come back with the man, and I'll give you twenty pennies . . . Come back with him in less than five minutes, and I'll give you forty! . . . **80**

(THE BOY IN HIS SUNDAY BEST vanishes like a shot from a gun. SCROOGE, then, talks to himself again.)

. . . I'll send it to Bob Cratchit's . . . He shan't know who sends it . . . It's twice the size of Tiny Tim . . . If it's too heavy to carry to Camden Town, they must have a cab . . . And . . . And . . . I'll PAY FOR IT! . . .

(SCROOGE looks round with a delighted smile. Coming towards him, he sees THE PORTLY GENTLEMAN who   **90** *called at his warehouse the day before. He takes THE PORTLY GENTLEMAN by both hands.)*

. . . My dear Sir! . . . How do you do? . . . I hope you were successful with your collection yesterday? . . . It was very kind of you . . . A Merry Christmas to you, Sir!

THE PORTLY GENTLEMAN	*(Mystified.)* Mr Scrooge?
SCROOGE	Yes! . . . That is my name, though I fear it may not be pleasant to you . . . Allow me to ask your pardon . . . And will you have the goodness to accept . . . A little **100** contribution . . .

(Here SCROOGE whispers in THE PORTLY GENTLEMAN'S ear.)

THE PORTLY GENTLEMAN	*(As if his breath has been taken away.)* Lord bless me! . . . My dear Mr Scrooge, are you serious?
SCROOGE	If you please . . . Not a penny less . . . A great many back-payments are included in it, I assure you . . . Will you do me that favour?
THE PORTLY GENTLEMAN	*(Shaking hands with SCROOGE.)* My dear Sir! . . . I don't know what to say to such munific . . .
SCROOGE	*(Interrupting him.)* Don't say anything, please! . . . Come and see me! . . . Will you come and see me?
THE PORTLY GENTLEMAN	I will! . . . I really mean that, I do! . . . I will!
SCROOGE	Thank 'ee! . . . I am much obliged to you . . . I thank you fifty times . . . Bless you! . . . And look who's here! . . .
	(Coming towards him, SCROOGE sees his nephew.)
	. . . Fred! . . . My nephew, Fred!
SCROOGE'S NEPHEW	Why, bless my soul, who's this?
SCROOGE	It is I . . . Your Uncle Scrooge . . . I want to come to dinner with you today, Fred . . . Will you let me in?
SCROOGE'S NEPHEW	Let you in? . . . Uncle Scrooge, *let you in?* . . .
	(FRED is so pleased at the idea, he nearly shakes his uncle's arm off.)
	. . . My! . . . We'll have a wonderful party! . . . We've waited *years* for you to come to us for Christmas . . . We'll have wonderful games . . . We'll all be wonderfully happy!
SCROOGE	And look who's coming here, now! . . .

110

120

munific . . . *The shocked portly gentleman was about to say munificence* meaning *splendid generosity.*

(Approaching him, SCROOGE sees BOB CRATCHIT. BOB   130
is carrying TINY TIM. Behind BOB and TIM, we see all
the other members of the CRATCHIT FAMILY.)

. . . Hello, Mr Cratchit! . . . And what do you mean by
being abroad at this time of day?

BOB CRATCHIT   *(Answering, by habit, in a timid way.)* I am very sorry,
Sir . . . I *am* behind my time.

SCROOGE   You are? . . . Yes, I think you are . . . Step this way, Sir
if you please.

BOB CRATCHIT   *(Pleading, again, by habit.)* It's only once a year, Sir! . . .
It shall not be repeated . . . I . . . tend . . . to . . . make   140
merry at Christmas, Sir.

SCROOGE   *(Sternly.)* Now I tell you what, my friend, I am not
going to stand this sort of thing any longer. And
therefore . . .

(He gives BOB CRATCHIT a dig in the waistcoat.)

. . . And therefore I am about to raise your salary! . . .

(BOB CRATCHIT, thinking that SCROOGE has gone mad,
is about to knock his employer down so that he can be
pinioned in a strait waistcoat, when SCROOGE continues
with an earnestness that can not be mistaken.)   150

. . . A Merry Christmas, Bob! . . . A merrier Christmas,
Bob my good fellow, than I have given you for many
a year! . . . I'll raise your salary, Bob! . . . I'll help you
to look after your family! . . . I'll be like a second
father to Tiny Tim! . . . I'll be as good a friend, as
good a master, and as good a man as this good old
city knows, or any other good old city, town or

---

      pinioned in a strait waistcoat *'restrained in a strait jacket'*

borough in the good old world . . . People will laugh, to see the alteration in me, but we'll not heed them! . . . Now! Let's have a party at my expense, eh? . . . The very best Christmas party there ever has been!

16(

CHARLES DICKENS   Nobody could be heartier, now, than Scrooge . . . Round him, there builds up a wonderful party . . . Wonderful games . . . Wonderful unanimity . . . Wonderful happiness!

(To the sound of joyful music, all present are swept up into an explosion of Christmas revelry . . . The youngsters dance round TINY TIM . . . FRED and OLD FEZZIWIG produce some extravagant Christmas decorations and hang them up . . . The other adults can dance, or enjoy themselves variously . . . Streamers are thrown, and unusual musical instruments are played . . . SCROOGE, at the centre of the festivities, is a man changed wonderfully by his recent experiences.)

17(

SCROOGE   *(Stopping the music, suddenly.)* Now! . . . Fill up your glasses with some hot and cheering punch, and I will ask you all to join me in a toast! . . .

(Liquid refreshments are quickly handed round.)

. . . May we all keep Christmas well! . . . This year, next year, and every year! . . . A Happy Christmas to us all!

18(

ALL OTHERS PRESENT   *(Raising their glasses.)* And so say all of us! . . . A Happy Christmas to us all!

TINY TIM   A Happy Christmas to us all . . . And, God bless us, every one!

---

 unanimity *'agreement from everyone there'*

ALL OTHERS PRESENT   *(And, possibly, the members of the audience.)* A Happy Christmas to us all . . . And, God bless us, every one!

(The Christmas bells ring out in a joyful carillon.)

 carillon *melody*

 IMPROVISATION: In a pair improvise the conversation between the poulterer and the boy Scrooge sends to him. Will he have any difficulty in persuading the poulterer that Mr Scrooge wishes to buy the prize turkey?

WRITING: Scrooge is wonderfully changed in this scene, so much so, that Bob thinks him mad! He makes a series of statements of intent – *I wills*. In a pair find and list these *I will* sentences. Add them to your spider diagram on the character of Scrooge. For example: *I will live in the past, the present, and the future!*

WRITING: Imagine that you are one of the Cratchit children. Write your diary entry of the best Christmas ever when Mr Scrooge raised your father's salary, sent your family an enormous turkey and arranged a last minute party.

EXPLORING LANGUAGE: The transformation of Scrooge is conveyed by exclamations and by his joyous repetitive language. Find and list all the examples of repetition in this scene. For example: *A bedpost! – My own bedpost!*

LOOKING BACK AT THE PLAY . . .

1 THE STORY AND THE PLAY

A Christmas Carol has a strong story line, a clear moral and memorable characters. It has been translated very successfully into a variety of media: radio and television adaptations, cartoon films and an animated musical version (*with The Muppets*).

Working in a small group, adapt the story to a comic strip format in 12 frames. One frame is given as an example below.

A CHRISTMAS CAROL

Now then. Are all the glasses filled?

The Cratchit family's sparse Christmas feast is assembled

You will need to decide carefully which clips of the story to select, agree on captions and write speech bubbles. Make sure at least one person in your group enjoys illustrating.

2 ARTWORK AND WRITING

When a play is performed, an accompanying programme is produced with a condensed version of the plot, a cast list and other snippets of interesting information.

In the same small group, design a theatre programme for *A Christmas Carol*. Try to use some quotation from the play and to design an interesting front cover. Use your school's IT facilities for a professional result. You could include your article about Christmas in the 1840's.

3 WRITING

Write a modern version of the story in about 300 words. For example, Scrooge might be a miserly millionaire with security guards and a private helicopter and the Cratchits might be desperately trying to send Tiny Tim to the United States for a special operation not available in this country.

4 WRITING

Imagine that you are one of the characters in the play. Write a chapter of your autobiography covering the events of the play. For example: *I shall never forget the Christmas of 1843 as long as I live. I went along as usual to visit my Uncle Scrooge in his counting house. The weather was cold and biting and . . .*

SCROOGE

5 DISCUSSION: THE TRANSFORMATION OF SCROOGE

Scrooge is the most important character in the play of *A Christmas Carol*. He appears in every scene and undergoes a startling transformation from wicked old screw to benevolent old gentleman.

In a small group collate and discuss all the information you have discovered about Scrooge in the form of lists and spider diagrams. Divide the information into two sets: Scrooge before the visit of the spectres and Scrooge on Christmas morning.

6 WRITING: SCROOGE'S LANGUAGE

It is easy to see that Scrooge has undergone a complete change in the final scene of the play not just because of his actions but also because of the language he uses. In the first scene, his favourite exclamations were, *Bah!* and *Humbug!* In the last scene, he calls out, *Glorious!* and *Bless you!*

Working in a small group, list examples of exclamations and strong statements made by Scrooge which reveal his character in the first and last scenes of the play. For example:

SCENE 1
Christmas! Ptchah! Christmas!
(In great disgust)

SCENE 6
I am as happy as an a angel!

7 WRITING: DICKENS'S PRESENTATION OF SCROOGE

Write an account of the character and conversion of Ebenezer Scrooge. Use all the information you have gathered from pair and group activities. Use quotations from the play to support the points you make.

For example: *At the beginning of the play, Scrooge is a heartless and mean old skinflint. I know this because Charles Dickens describes him as, 'Hard and sharp as flint' and as 'a covetous old sinner'.*

8 WRITING AND ACTING: AN EXTRA SCENE

Work in a small group to add an extra scene to the end of the play. Use your knowledge of the story and the characters. Remind yourself of the language the characters use and of the need for stage directions. Prepare your scene for performance. Learn lines, practise and decide on props and costumes. Be prepared to perform to the rest of the class.

9 EVALUATING AND DRAFTING: AN EXTRA SCENE

Make notes on the scenes and performances of other groups. Write an evaluation of each performance under the headings:

script, acting *(voice, gesture, movement, characterisation)*,
costumes and props.

Evaluate your own script and performance. Produce a final, improved version of your scene.

10 WRITING: THE LANGUAGE OF DICKENS

Write an account of the kind of language used in the play version of *A Christmas Carol*. To prepare your account, re-read what you wrote in response to the Exploring Language activities 1, 5 and 6, and in response to activity 6 above.

Remember the non standard language used by some characters and the high number of exclamations as well as the more descriptive speeches. Quote examples of language to support the points you make. Part of your answer might look like this: *The character, Charles Dickens, uses very descriptive language when he introduces Scrooge. Firstly he tells us that Scrooge is 'tight-fisted'.*